GARDEN GUIDES

PRUNING

GARDEN GUIDES

PRUNING

ANTHONY BROOKS

Illustrations by
BRENDA STEPHENSON

CHARTWELL
BOOKS, INC.

Published by Chartwell Books
a division of Book Sales, Inc.
114 Northfield Avenue
Edison, NJ 08837

This edition produced for sale
in the U.S.A., its territories
and dependencies only.

Text and artwork copyright © Parragon Book Service Ltd 1996
Photographs copyright © Robert Ditchfield Ltd 1996
This edition copyright © Parragon Book Service Ltd 1996

ISBN 0-7858-0533-8

Produced by Robert Ditchfield Ltd

Printed and bound in Italy

CONTENTS

Poisonous Plants

In recent years, concern has been voiced about poisonous plants or plants which can cause allergic reactions if touched. The fact is that many plants are poisonous, some in a particular part, others in all their parts. For the sake of safety, it is always, without exception, essential to assume that no part of a plant should be eaten unless it is known, without any doubt whatsoever, that the plant or its part is edible and that it cannot provoke an allergic reaction in the individual person who samples it. It must also be remembered that some plants can cause severe dermatitis, blistering or an allergic reaction if touched, in some individuals and not in others. It is the responsibility of the individual to take all the above into account.

How to Use This Book

The first chapter (pages 15–19) explains the procedures that are used throughout the book and the reasons for them, so that when you read, for example, 'hard prune' you know what to do and why. Subsequent chapters give advice on when and how to prune individual genera and species, many of which are illustrated with photographs to help you identify them. The glossary on page 78 defines certain words which are used to identify parts of plants or which are terms commonly used to explain pruning procedures.

The following symbols are also used where appropriate:

D = deciduous
E = evergreen

Plant Names

For ease of reference this book gives the botanical name under which a plant is most widely listed for the gardener. Common names are given wherever they are in frequent use and these are cross-referenced in the index.

PRUNING

LEFT TO THEIR OWN DEVICES, many shrubs would become overgrown tangled thickets. Pruning is essential to keep plants looking their best. But pruning is not just a case of tidying up; it can make an important contribution to the success of your garden. Besides restricting the size of large shrubs, pruning will promote larger flowers in profusion and fruit trees will crop heavily with better quality fruit. Trees like willows may be coppiced for striking winter stems. Ailanthus might be pollarded for dramatic foliage effect. Understanding pruning will enable you to get the best performance through the year from your plants.

MAINTAIN HEALTH AND VIGOUR
Thinning out branches to allow light and air into shrubs and trees will often stimulate healthy growth. An open framework of branches is less likely to be infected with diseases or pests. Always remove dead and diseased wood.

IMPROVE ORNAMENTAL EFFECT
Flowers and Fruit Unpruned plants will lose vigour and as a result flowers and fruit will become smaller. Pruning diverts energy

The rose 'Raubritter' beautifully shaped to produce a mass of blooms by a small pool.

Huge leaves on a hard pruned *Paulownia tomentosa*.

into the production of larger and better fruit or flowers.

Coloured stems The vividly coloured stems of dogwoods and willows can be achieved by hard pruning each year.

Foliage effect The foliage of many shrubs can be enhanced by hard pruning annually, promoting dramatically large leaves or intensely coloured foliage.

TRAIN TO THE SHAPE REQUIRED

If left unpruned, shrubs will often develop into a confused, shapeless tangle. Judicious

The bright stems of the dogwood *Cornus alba*.

Clipped box and ivy make a charming feature on a terrace.

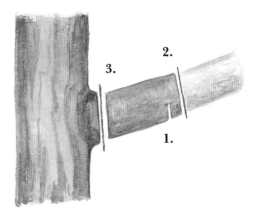

REMOVING A BRANCH

Large branches should be cut into sections, otherwise the branch may fall when cutting, tearing the wood.

1. Undercut the branch 30cm/12in from the trunk, cutting through a quarter of the branch.

2. Make a top cut a little further on. Continue cutting until the branch falls.

3. Finally cut back the stump just outside the branch collar.

pruning will improve their shape, encouraging a compact habit and will ensure that older stems are replaced by free-flowering stems.

HOW TO PRUNE

Sharp cutting tools are vital to produce clear pruning cuts. Ragged cuts may result in dieback and disease. Secateurs should be used for cutting shoots or small branches up to about 2.5cm/1in thick. For larger branches, use long-handled pruners or a pruning saw.

Prune back to a bud or shoot pointing in the desired direction of growth. Avoid pruning to inward-growing buds or shoots that may cross or rub against each other.

Always cut out dead, diseased or damaged wood completely and remove all weak, crossing or badly-placed stems. Aim to produce an open-centred bush.

Cutting off branches flush with the trunk may look more attractive but this is damaging to the tree since it takes far longer for the wound to heal. It is better to angle the cut so that the branch bark ridge and branch collar are left untouched. The branch bark ridge is a swelling of rough bark around a branch where it joins the trunk.

11

A Seasonal Guide to Pruning

This table must be used in conjunction with the entries on individual species in this book.

SPRING
– Prune late-summer flowering shrubs, such as *Buddleja davidii*, ceanothus (deciduous types), ceratostigma, fuchsia, hydrangea, hypericum, lavatera, leycesteria, *Spiraea douglasii*.
– Prune Hybrid Tea, Floribunda and Climbing roses.
– Renovate overgrown shrubs and hedges.
– Hard prune certain *Cornus*, *Rubus* and *Salix* species.
– Pollard or coppice willows, poplars, eucalyptus, paulownia and ailanthus.
– Prune clematis and other climbers.
– Prune sub-shrubs such as santolina and caryopteris back to new growth.
– Clip over *Calluna*, *Daboecia* and summer-flowering *Erica* species.
– Prune spring-flowering shrubs after flowering – forsythia, *Jasminum nudiflorum*, *Lonicera × purpusii* and *Prunus triloba*.
– Prune peaches, nectarines, cherries, plums and gages.

SUMMER
– Prune summer-flowering shrubs after flowering – *Buddleja alternifolia*, deutzia, kolkwitzia, philadelphus, *Rubus tridel*, syringa and weigela.
– Summer prune wisteria.
– Dead-head rhododendrons.
– Summer prune trained fruit trees.
– Summer prune gooseberries, red and white currants.
– Dead-head roses regularly.
– Clip hedges regularly throughout the summer.
– Tie in and train wall shrubs. Shorten breastwood.
– Remove water shoots on trees.
– Prune peaches, nectarines, cherries, plums and gages.

AUTUMN
– Prune rose bushes – shorten long stems to reduce wind rock.
– Prune Rambler roses – remove flowered stems.
– Prune autumn-fruiting raspberries, blackberries, hybrid berries and blackcurrants.
– Prune trees which are susceptible to bleeding, such as acers, horse chestnut, birches, laburnum and robinia.

WINTER
– Prune wisteria, actinidia and vines.
– Remove branches from trees throughout winter if necessary.
– Winter prune apples and pears.
– Prune gooseberries, blueberries, red and white currants.
– Prune autumn-fruiting raspberries to ground level.

When to Prune

Pruning times are usually determined by the reasons for pruning and the specific needs of each plant. However, other practical reasons should be considered.

Early pruning stimulates soft new growth which may be killed by frost and cold winds. Sub-shrubs, such as fuchsia, hebe and ceratostigma, should be pruned in late spring when new growth appears. Old growth should be left intact over winter to provide some frost protection.

Conifers should be pruned in autumn to avoid bleeding. Evergreen shrubs should be pruned in spring.

Some plants are susceptible to diseases and therefore pruning should be carried out when plants are less likely to be at risk of infection. Cherries, plums and other prunus species affected by silver leaf disease should be pruned in summer when they are less vulnerable to infection.

Certain plants, such as acer (maple), betula (birch) and vitis (vine) bleed badly from pruning cuts; this may cause die-back and reduce vigour. Such plants are best pruned in the autumn when the sap is not rising. Walnuts on the other hand should be pruned in early summer.

TOOLS OF THE TRADE

Crushed stems and ragged cuts may die back and become infected with disease. It is therefore essential that sharp clean tools are used when pruning to give clean cuts.

SECATEURS

The most useful pruning tool. Select a strong pair which you find comfortable to handle. Use secateurs for branches up to about 2.5cm/1in thick. Never try to cut larger branches since this may twist the blades of the secateurs and damage the stems of the plant.

LONG-HANDLED PRUNERS (LOPPERS)

Use loppers for branches up to 5cm/2in thick. The long handles enable easy pruning of thorny subjects, such as roses.

SHEARS

Shears can be used for clipping shrubs and topiary to shape and for trimming hedges. Heathers and helianthemums may be clipped over with shears for dead-heading (removing dead flowers).

SAWS

Saws are necessary for cutting branches over 5cm/2in thick. Straight pruning saws are mainly used for small branches in confined spaces where loppers cannot be used. Curved Grecian saws are easy to use in difficult places and make good clean cuts. Bow saws like the one shown here are generally used for sawing large branches and logs.

TREE PRUNERS

Tree pruners mounted on a long pole are useful for removing high branches without a ladder.

1. Pruning Techniques

The result you are aiming for is the main factor in deciding on the technique.

PRUNING TECHNIQUES

FORMATIVE PRUNING

Formative pruning is necessary to ensure young plants develop a good framework of well-spaced branches. This will lead to the shrub developing a balanced shape. Remove weak, crossing and overcrowded branches. Aim to create an open centred bush, as with the spiraea shown on the right.

CUTTING TO SHAPE

Some shrubs have a compact habit which can be maintained by cutting back to shape. Larger leaved plants, such as laurel and aucuba should be pruned to shape with secateurs. Small leaved shrubs, such as *Lonicera nitida* (*above*) and *Buxus* (box), should be clipped to shape with shears.

RENEWAL PRUNING

Renewal pruning maintains a constant supply of new shoots, otherwise the shrub would become cluttered with old and dead branches. Remove dead and diseased branches at ground level. Aim to cut out a third of the oldest stems. Feed and mulch after flowering.This technique is used for two groups of deciduous shrubs.

SPRING-FLOWERING SHRUBS
These shrubs flower in late winter and spring on shoots of the previous year's growth. Prune after flowering. Examples: forsythia, *Jasminum nudiflorum*, *Berberis darwinii*.

SUMMER-FLOWERING SHRUBS
These shrubs flower in summer on shoots of the previous year's growth. Prune after flowering. Examples: philadelphus, deutzia, weigela (*left*), kolkwitzia, kerria, *Buddleja alternifolia*.

REDUCING GROWTH

This technique prevents cytisus and genista (both commonly called broom) becoming straggly and overgrown; it promotes new growth and compact habit. After flowering, cut two-thirds of flowered wood back to new growth. Do not cut into the old wood.

RENOVATION

Occasionally shrubs may outgrow their situation, become neglected or simply lose vigour. Renovation avoids the need to remove the shrub unless the plant is badly diseased or damaged.

DECIDUOUS SHRUBS
In winter, remove all dead and diseased wood and cut back a third of the old stems to ground level. Remove twiggy growth. Feed, mulch and water to stimulate new growth. New stems will develop and the remaining old stems should be cut out the following year. Old forsythias (*right*) can be treated in this way.

EVERGREENS
Many evergreens can be renovated by hard pruning all stems to within 30–45cm/12–18in of ground level in late spring. Feed, mulch and water after pruning to encourage new growth to develop.

PRUNING TECHNIQUES

ROOT PRUNING

Root pruning is occasionally used to restrict the growth of vigorous trees or shrubs. It can also help to stimulate improved fruiting and flowering. In early spring dig a trench 30–60 cm/12–24in deep beyond the spread of the branch canopy. Prune back thick roots but retain fibrous roots. Replace the soil and firm.

NO REGULAR PRUNING

Some shrubs require minimal pruning once established except for the removal of dead, diseased and damaged shoots.

DEAD-HEADING

Removing faded flowers or unripe seed pods improves the appearance of a plant and encourages more flowers to develop. Heathers clipped with shears after flowering will remain compact and neat. Rhododendrons benefit from dead-heading; carefully snap off flowerheads between finger and thumb.

PRUNING TECHNIQUES

HARD PRUNING (COPPICING)

Hard pruning is the annual pruning of a tree or shrub to ground level resulting in the production of a quantity of vigorous basal growth.

FOLIAGE EFFECT

Hard pruning may be used to improve the foliage effect of some shrubs. Cotinus, *Rhus typhina, Corylus maxima* 'Purpurea' and elders (*above*) respond by producing rapid growth.

JUVENILE FOLIAGE

If you prune eucalyptus to about 30cm/12in from the ground in the spring, this will give a shrubby habit and attractive foliage.

ORNAMENTAL STEMS

Hard pruning of shrubs with striking stems, such as willows, dogwoods (*Cornus alba* is shown here before and after pruning), white stemmed brambles and leycesteria, stimulates strong, new, brightly coloured stems. Feed and mulch after pruning.

SUB-SHRUBS

Many sub-shrubs respond to hard pruning since they quickly become straggly. Regular cutting back encourages a neat compact habit. Leave stems over winter to give frost protection and cut back to new growth after the danger of frost has passed. Do not cut back into old wood. Examples: hypericum (*left*), santolina, fuchsia.

IMPROVED FLOWERS

Some flowering shrubs like *Buddleja davidii* (shown here before and after pruning) and *Hydrangea paniculata* will produce larger flowerheads if hard pruned. Cut back to buds about 5cm/2in from the old wood in spring.

POLLARDING

Pollarding is the regular cutting back of branches to a stem or framework in early spring. In the past this method provided a regular supply of poles and firewood. In gardens pollarding may be used to restrict a tree's size, to enhance foliage effect or to produce decorative winter stems.

The stems that shoot from some willows when they are pollarded are particularly attractive. The sequence of pictures on this page shows the pollarding of the willow *Salix alba vitellina* 'Britzensis' by a small pond.
For foliage effect, pollard ailanthus, paulownias and poplars; the resulting leaves will be dramatically larger than if these trees had not been treated. Eucalyptus will retain its attractive juvenile foliage when pollarded.

Trees for pollarding: *Acer pensylvanicum* 'Erythrocladum', *A. negundo* 'Flamingo', cornus, eucalyptus, salix (willow), populus (poplar), ailanthus, paulownia, tilia (lime), platanus (plane).

2. SHRUBS AND TREES

An A–Z listing of ornamental plants and their pruning requirements.

SHRUBS

YOUNG FLOWERING SHRUBS should be pruned regularly in the initial stages. Remove overcrowded, crossing and badly-placed shoots to establish a well-balanced framework. Once this framework has been achieved, most shrubs require little pruning except to remove unwanted branches. However, there are some plants that need regular pruning to produce the best effect.

Evergreen shrubs are also included in this section. These require little pruning except for the removal of dead and diseased wood or to improve their shape. Cut back any winter damage in spring. Some evergreens, like laurel and rhododendron, respond to hard pruning in spring.

Abelia No regular pruning. Thin out old wood after flowering. Remove winter damaged growth in spring. D or E.

Amelanchier (Snowy mespilus) No regular pruning. If necessary, remove old and damaged branches in winter.

Aralia (Angelica tree) No regular pruning. Remove suckers in spring.

Aucuba Remove reversion, dead and diseased branches. Responds to hard pruning. For a compact plant, shorten shoots. E

Berberis (Barberry) Prune evergreens after flowering. Deciduous species should have old and damaged branches removed in spring.

Buddleja alternifolia Prune flowered branches back to strong new shoots immediately after flowering. Aim to remove ⅔ of growth.

Buddleja davidii (Butterfly bush) Hard prune back to 5cm/2in from the old wood in early spring.

Buddleja globosa Prune lightly after flowering.

Buxus (Box) Clip to shape, mid–late summer. Leggy specimens may be rejuvenated by hard pruning in spring. E

Camellia Little pruning. Dead-head after flowering. Cut back frost damaged shoots to new growth. Shorten straggly growths in spring. E

Ceanothus (Californian lilac) Deciduous types: shorten previous year's growth back to 7.5–10cm/3–4in in spring. Evergreen types: no regular pruning.

Ceratostigma (Hardy plumbago) Cut back all stems to ground level in spring. D or E.

SHRUBS

Chaenomeles (Japanese quince) Thin out crowded branches after flowering. If wall trained, prune previous year's growth back to two or three buds.

Chimonanthus (Winter sweet) Thin out old and crowded branches after flowering. Wall shrubs should have flowered stems shortened by half.

Choisya (Mexican orange blossom) No regular pruning. Shorten frosted shoots back to healthy foliage in spring. Overgrown shrubs may be hard pruned. E

Clerodendrum Hard prune *C. bungei* (shown here) back to new growth in spring. *C. trichotomum* requires no regular pruning.

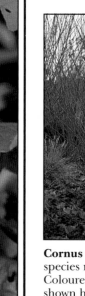

Cornus (Dogwood) Tree species require no pruning. Coloured bark types (*C. alba* shown here) should be hard pruned annually in spring.

Cotinus (Smoke bush) If grown as a flowering shrub, only limited pruning is necessary. If grown for foliage, hard prune in spring.

Cotoneaster Pruning is only needed to restrict growth. Remove damaged branches in spring. D or E

Cytisus (Broom) After flowering, shorten the previous year's growth by half. Avoid pruning old wood. D or E.

Deutzia After flowering, remove old flowered stems and cut out dead wood.

Daphne Daphnes are best left unpruned. Straggly growths may be removed in spring. D or E

Elaeagnus Prune to shape in spring. Remove suckers and reversion (when variegated leaves revert to green, as shown here). As hedges, shorten individual branches in summer. E

SHRUBS

Escallonia Cut back old branches to vigorous shoots after flowering. Remove frost damage and dead wood in spring. (See also Hedges.) E

Euonymus No regular pruning. Cut out reverted shoots. Clip hedges in spring and again in late summer if necessary. E.

Exochorda No regular pruning. Overcrowded stems and old wood may be removed after flowering.

Fatsia (False castor oil plant) No regular pruning. Hard prune old branches to ground level in spring. E

Forsythia After flowering, remove several old branches down to ground level. Thin out crowded shoots from centre.

Fuchsia Cut back all stems to ground level in spring. In mild areas, simply cut back winter damage.

Garrya (Tassel bush) Pruning is seldom necessary except to restrict size. Cut back stems in spring. E

Hibiscus No regular pruning. Remove dead or damaged stems in spring.

Genista (Broom) No regular pruning. Light clipping after flowering will encourage bushy growth. Do not cut into old wood.

Hamamelis (Witch hazel) No regular pruning. To restrict growth, prune lightly after flowering. Suckers should be removed.

Hebe (Veronica) No regular pruning. Prune frost damaged growth back to new shoots in spring. Dead-head throughout the flowering season. E

SHRUBS

Hippophaë (Sea buckthorn) Requires no regular pruning. If it is necessary to restrict growth, prune in spring.

Hydrangea Remove dead flower heads from *H. macrophylla* varieties in spring. *H. paniculata* requires hard pruning. Other types require little pruning.

Hypericum (St John's wort) Hard prune *H. calycinum* (shown above) and *H.x inodorum* to ground level in spring. Other types, prune back to new growth. D or E

Indigofera (Indigo bush) Cut back frost damaged shoots to new growth. Alternatively, hard prune all stems to ground level in spring.

Kalmia (Calico bush) No regular pruning. Dead-head after flowering. Old bushes may be rejuvenated by hard pruning in spring. E

Kerria Cut out old canes to ground level after flowering.

Kolkwitzia (Beauty bush) After flowering remove old flowered stems and weak growth at ground level.

Leptospermum No regular pruning. Remove frost damage and straggly branches in spring. E

Lavatera (Mallow) In autumn, shorten shoots by half to reduce wind damage. Hard prune all stems in spring. E

Leucothoë No regular pruning. Remove old and weak stems at ground level in spring. E

Leycesteria (Pheasant berry) In spring, cut back old and weak shoots to ground level. May also be hard pruned.

Lonicera (Honeysuckle) Shrubby honeysuckles require no regular pruning. Remove old and weak growth in spring. (See also Climbers and Hedges.) D or E

Magnolia No regular pruning. Remove damaged or unwanted branches in midsummer. D or E

Mahonia *M. aquifolium* may be hard pruned in spring. Other species require no regular pruning. Remove damaged growth in spring. E

Olearia (Daisy bush) Frost damaged growth should be pruned back to new shoots in spring. Olearias will tolerate hard pruning. E

Osmanthus No regular pruning. Prune to shape after flowering. Overgrown shrubs may be hard pruned. Clip hedges in spring. E

Ozothamnus No regular pruning. Prune frost damaged stems back to new growth in spring. E

Paeonia (Tree peony) No regular pruning. Remove dead shoots in early summer.

Pernettya (syn. Gaultheria, Prickly heath) No regular pruning. Prune oldest stems to ground level in spring. E

Perovskia (Russian sage)
Hard prune all stems close
to ground level in spring.

Philadelphus (Mock orange)
Immediately after flowering, prune
old branches down to ground level
to stimulate new growth.

Phlomis (Jerusalem sage)
Dead-head after flowering.
Cut back old and frost
damaged stems to new
growth in spring. E

Photinia Shortening shoots
in summer encourages new
foliage and compact
growth. Cut back overgrown
plants in spring. E

Pieris Remove frost damage
in spring. Remove dead
flowers. Overgrown plants
may be hard pruned to
ground level. E

Pittosporum Prune to
shape in spring, removing
winter damage.
Pittosporums respond to
hard pruning in spring. E

Potentilla (Cinquefoil) In spring, remove dead or old stems at ground level. Shorten the previous year's growth by half.

Prunus (Cherry) Hard prune *P. glandulosa* and *P. triloba* close to ground level in spring. *P. tenella* (above) requires no regular pruning.

Pyracantha (Firethorn) After flowering, shorten breastwood by 7.5–10cm/3–4in. Cut hedges in summer. E

Rhus (Sumach) No regular pruning but, for foliage effect only, prune *R. glabra* (above) and *R. typhina* to ground level in early spring.

Rhododendron Pruning is not essential. Old leggy plants may be hard pruned in spring. Break off faded flowers. E

33

SHRUBS

Ribes (Flowering currant) Remove old branches at ground level, annually, in spring.

Rubus (Bramble) Decorative stem types: hard prune annually in spring. Flowering types: remove old branches at ground level after flowering.

Salix (Willow) Coloured bark varieties are pollarded annually in early spring. Other types: remove dead or diseased branches.

Sarcococca (Sweet box) Requires little pruning. Cut dead or old stems to ground level in spring. E

Senecio (syn. Brachyglottis) No regular pruning. Cut back winter damage, old and straggly shoots in spring. Senecios respond to hard pruning. E

Sambucus (Elder) Remove oldest stems to ground level in spring. Varieties grown for their foliage should be hard pruned annually.

Skimmia No regular pruning. Overgrown bushes may be hard pruned in spring. E

SHRUBS

Sorbaria Remove a third of the oldest stems at ground level in spring.

Spiraea Spring-flowering types: remove old stems after flowering. Summer-flowering varieties: hard prune to 10–12cm/4–5in from ground level in spring.

Syringa (Lilac) Remove oldest branches in winter. Neglected plants respond to hard pruning. Dead-head after flowering. Remove suckers.

Tamarix (Tamarisk) *T. tetrandra*: shorten shoots by half after flowering. *T. pentandra*: shorten last year's growth by half in spring.

Viburnum No regular pruning. Remove old or damaged branches from evergreen types in spring and from deciduous types after flowering.

Weigela After flowering, prune several old stems back to ground level. Weigelas will respond to hard pruning.

TREES

FORMATIVE PRUNING OF YOUNG TREES ensures that they develop an attractive well balanced shape. However, the pruning needed will depend upon the type of tree selected: feathered, multi-stemmed or standard. Once the framework is established, trees need minimal pruning except for the removal of dead, diseased or damaged branches. Most trees should be pruned when dormant in late autumn and winter. Trees susceptible to bleeding should be pruned from late summer to autumn.

BRANCHED-HEAD STANDARD

Cut back the central leader when the desired height is reached. Allow four or five well positioned branches to develop a branching head.

FEATHERED TREE

Cut out crossing, overcrowded and badly positioned branches which spoil the shape of the tree. Remove competing leaders.

MULTI-STEMMED

Prune a young plant down to 30cm/12in from ground level. Then allow only four or five well placed stems to develop.

CENTRAL-LEADER STANDARD

Remove competing leaders. Cut back all lowest branches gradually as the tree develops, until the desired length of clear trunk is reached.

TREES

BLEEDING

Some trees, like maples (*Acer*), birches (*Betula*) and hornbeams (*Carpinus*), bleed excessively if they are pruned in early spring. This causes die-back and weakens the tree. To avoid this problem, prune them in late summer to autumn.

EPICORMIC OR WATER SHOOTS

These are vigorous shoots that often grow around old pruning wounds. Remove epicormics as soon as they appear, cutting them back as close to the trunk as possible.

Maple (*Acer*) Train as central-leader standards or feathered trees. No regular pruning. Prune in autumn to avoid bleeding.

Horse chestnut (*Aesculus*) Train as central-leader standards. No regular pruning.

Alder (*Alnus*) No regular pruning. Train as a central-leader standard or a feathered tree. Remove epicormic growth.

Strawberry tree (*Arbutus*) No regular pruning. Can regenerate if hard pruned in spring. *A. menziesii* should be trained with a clear trunk.

Birch (*Betula*) Train as a central-leader standard or multi-stemmed tree. Prune in late summer to autumn to avoid bleeding.

Hornbeam (*Carpinus*) No regular pruning. Train as a central-leader standard. Prune in winter to avoid bleeding.

Sweet chestnut (*Castanea*) Train as a central-leader standard. No regular pruning. Remove epicormic growth.

Indian bean tree (*Catalpa*) Train as a branched-head standard. No regular pruning. Hard prune Indian bean trees in mid-spring for foliage effect.

Judas tree (*Cercis*) Train as a branched-head standard. No routine pruning. Remove dead or damaged shoots in early summer.

Hazel (*Corylus*) Remove old branches at ground level in autumn. Coppice *C. avellana* forms annually in spring for foliage effect. Treat Turkish hazel (*C. colurna*) as a central-leader standard.

Hawthorn (*Crataegus*) Train as a central-leader standard or branched-head standard.

No regular pruning. Remove epicormic growth.

Eucalyptus Train as multi-stemmed trees or central-leader standards. No regular pruning. Coppice in spring to retain juvenile foliage.

Beech (*Fagus*) No regular pruning. Treat as a central-leader standard. See also Hedges.

Ash (*Fraxinus*) Train as a central-leader standard. No regular pruning.

Honey locust (*Gleditsia*) Train as branched-head standards or central-leader standards. No regular pruning. If necessary prune in late summer.

Holly (*Ilex*) No regular pruning. If necessary, prune in early spring. Remove reverted shoots on variegated forms.

Walnut (*Juglans*) Train as a central-leader standard. Avoid pruning if possible. Prune only in late summer to avoid bleeding.

Pride of India (*Koelreuteria*) Train as a central-leader standard. No regular pruning.

Golden rain (*Laburnum*) Train as a central-leader standard or branched-head standard. No regular pruning. Prune in summer to avoid bleeding.

Sweet gum (*Liquidambar*) Train as a central-leader standard. No regular pruning.

Tulip tree (*Liriodendron*) Train as a central-leader standard. No regular pruning. Remove competing leaders.

Crab apple (*Malus*) Train as a branched-head standard or central-leader standard. No regular pruning. Remove suckers and epicormic growth.

Medlar (*Mespilus*) Train as a branched-head standard. No regular pruning. Remove epicormic growth.

Mulberry (*Morus*) Train as a central-leader standard. prune in late summer as mulberries bleed badly.

Persian ironwood (*Parrotia*) Train as a branched-head standard tree or allow it to develop as a large shrub. No regular pruning.

Foxglove tree (*Paulownia*) Train as a central-leader standard. No regular pruning. Alternatively, coppice to ground level in spring for foliage effect.

Plane (*Platanus*) Train as central-leader standards. No regular pruning. Trees may be pollarded in winter.

TREES

SUCKERS

Suckers develop around budded or grafted trees. These will weaken and eventually dominate the plant. Pull them out or cut them back as close to the stem or root as possible.

SILVER LEAF DISEASE

Silver leaf disease can affect all members of the prunus family, causing die-back or complete death. Pruning in summer lessens the risk of infection.

Poplar (*Populus*) Train as a central-leader standard or feathered tree. Pollard *P. candicans* 'Aurora' in winter for foliage effect.

Cherry (*Prunus*) Train as a central-leader standard. No regular pruning. Prune in early summer to avoid silver leaf disease.

Pear (*Pyrus*) Train as a central-leader standard. No regular pruning. Train *P. salicifolia* 'Pendula' as a branched-head tree.

Oak (*Quercus*) Train as a central-leader standard or feathered tree. No regular pruning.

False acacia (*Robinia*) Generally grown as central-leader standards. Remove competing leaders and suckers. Prune in late summer to avoid bleeding.

Willow (*Salix*) Train as central-leader standards. Alternatively, pollard or coppice in spring. Remove dead and diseased wood in winter.

Mountain ash and **Whitebeam** (*Sorbus* spp.) Generally grown as central-leader standard trees. No regular pruning. If necessary, prune in mid-spring.

Lime (*Tilia*) Train as central-leader standards. Prune in late summer. Remove epicormic growth. Limes may be pollarded or pleached.

Elm (*Ulmus*) Train as a central-leader standard. No regular pruning. Remove

CONIFERS

Conifers generally require very little pruning. Dead branches should be cut back to the trunk. Most conifers will not tolerate severe pruning into old wood.

Conifers bleed excessively if pruned in spring and summer and should therefore be pruned in autumn to avoid this problem.

Train conifers so that they have a single central leader (the leading top shoot). If rival leaders develop, cut out the competing leader right back to its point of origin.

Some conifers with coloured or variegated foliage are prone to revert to their plain colour and produce all-green shoots. Cut these out as soon as possible.

3. FRUIT

Pruning of fruit trees should be a regular operation to ensure abundant cropping.

APPLES *and* PEARS

ROUTINE PRUNING OF FRUIT TREES is necessary in the early stages to form a framework of branches and maintain tree shape, and later to ensure a balance between new growth and fruit production.

ESTABLISHED BUSHES

Only winter pruning is needed for established bushes. The pruning needed will depend on the variety. Varieties which bear fruit on the tips of the shoots are called 'tip bearers'. Other varieties develop fruit on spurs – these are called 'spur bearers'.

TIP-BEARING VARIETIES Prune all branch leaders by about a third. Leave all sideshoots with fruit buds at their tips unpruned. Vigorous sideshoots may be shortened by half. Remove dead, crowded and crossing branches, aim to keep the centre open.

SPUR-BEARING VARIETIES Cut back sideshoots to three or six buds. Prune leaders by one third to an outward-facing bud. Remove dead, crossing and crowded branches. Keep the centre open.

FORMING A CORDON

After planting a feathered maiden, shorten all sideshoots over 10cm/4in long to three buds. Leave the leader unpruned.

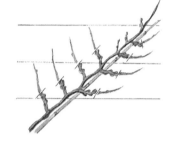

Begin summer-pruning of established cordons once shoots have developed woody bases. Shorten laterals back to three leaves beyond the basal cluster and cut back sub-laterals to one leaf beyond the basal cluster. When the leader reaches the required height, shorten it back to 15cm/6in above the top wire.

FORMING AN OPEN-CENTRED BUSH

1. Begin with a feathered maiden tree. In winter prune the leader to a lateral shoot 75cm/2½ft above ground level, leaving four evenly spaced laterals below. Shorten these by about half their length to an outward-facing bud. Remove all other shoots.

2. In the following winter shorten vigorous shoots by one third and weak shoots should be pruned by half to outward-facing buds. Remove dead, crossing and damaged shoots.

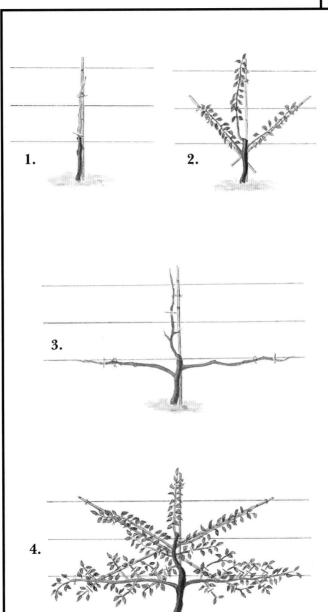

1.

2.

3.

4.

FORMING AN ESPALIER

1. Prune a maiden tree back to a good bud 5cm/2in above the first wire.

2. In summer train the leading shoot to a cane as it develops. Train two side branches to canes at an angle of 45°. Shorten any other sideshoots to three leaves.

3. In late autumn tie down the arms of the first tier. Prune the leader to a bud, just above the second wire. Shorten other sideshoots to three buds.

4. In the second summer train the leader vertically and the two lateral branches at 45°. Shorten all other sideshoots to three leaves.
Repeat this method until the required number of tiers has been formed. Prune back the leader in winter to just above the top tier.

ESTABLISHED ESPALIER TREES

In mid to late summer shorten laterals back to three leaves and sub-laterals to one leaf.

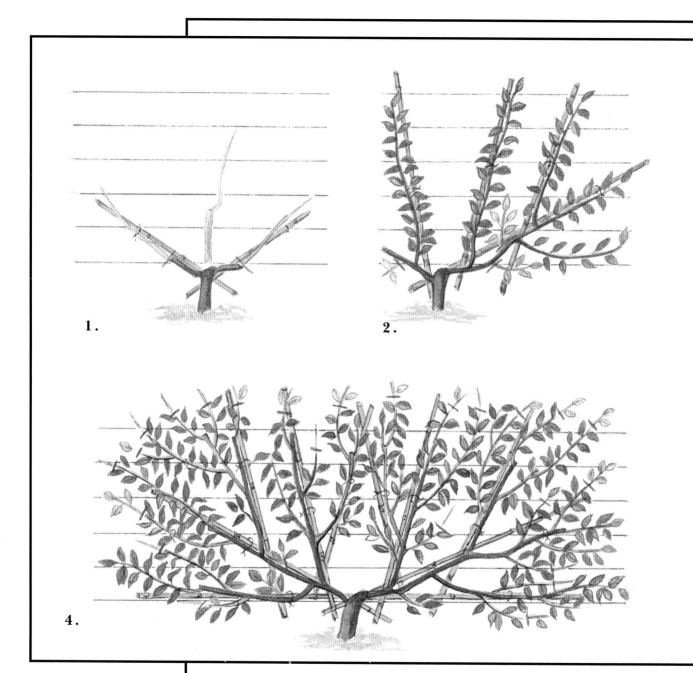

1.

2.

4.

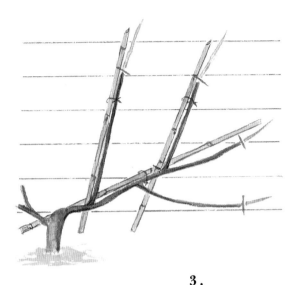

3.

FORMING A PEACH OR NECTARINE FAN

1. In early spring cut back a feathered maiden to two well-placed laterals, one on each side, 30cm/12in above the ground. Prune each lateral to 38cm/15in from the main stem. This will stimulate sideshoots to form on the lowest branches of the fan.
2. In the second summer select four shoots on each of the laterals to develop, two sideshoots on the upper side, one on the underside and one to extend the leader. Pinch back all other shoots to one leaf. Train the selected sideshoots onto canes attached to wires.
3. In the third spring shorten leaders by one third to strong upward-pointing buds.
4. In the third summer train in new shoots until all space is filled. Pinch out unwanted shoots.

PRUNING ESTABLISHED FAN-TRAINED PEACHES

In late spring prune one year old shoots. Leave replacement shoots at the base unpruned and reduce all other shoots to a single leaf. Shoots which grow from main framework branches should be thinned out to 15cm/6in apart.

After fruiting prune each fruited stem back to a replacement shoot near its base. Tie in the replacement shoots to fill the space.

PLUMS AND GAGES are normally grown as half-standards with 1.2m/4ft trunks or fan-trained against warm walls.

FORMING A HALF-STANDARD PLUM

1. Plant a maiden tree in winter. In spring prune the leader to 1.2m/4ft above the ground.

2. The following summer select four or five strong branches. Shorten back all other shoots to four leaves – this will help to thicken the stem.

3. In the second spring prune the main branches back by half to an outward-facing bud. Remove all other sideshoots.

4. In the third spring select eight main branches to develop. Prune these back by a half to outward-facing buds. Shorten sideshoots growing in the centre to 10cm/4in. Remove crossing and weak shoots.

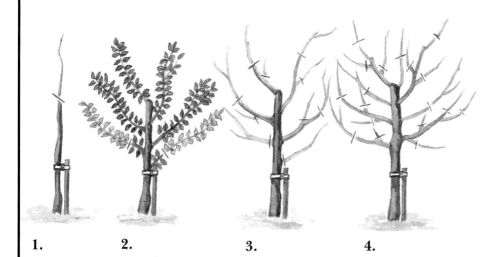

1.   **2.**   **3.**   **4.**

FAN-TRAINED PLUMS

Train and prune plum fans as for peach fans.

PRUNING ESTABLISHED PLUMS

Once the framework is formed, plums require very little pruning. Remove dead, diseased or damaged branches. Thin out overcrowded branches in the centre. Always prune in summer to reduce the risk of silver leaf infection.

CHERRIES   Prune cherries in late spring or summer, when there is less risk of infection from silver leaf or bacterial canker. Cut out any branches which show signs of these diseases as soon as possible. In small gardens, cherries are best grown as fans on a wall or fence.

ACID CHERRY FANS are trained in the same way as peach fans. Once the framework has been established, the fan is renewal pruned to ensure a constant supply of young growth.
In early summer thin out new shoots to 10cm/4in apart. Remove outward or ingrowing shoots.
After harvesting, cut back each fruited stem to a replacement shoot at its base.

SWEET CHERRIES are pruned and trained like peach fans. In summer, cut back sideshoots to six leaves. In autumn, shorten these sideshoots again, cutting back to three buds. Remove all outward or ingrowing shoots.

Sweet cherry 'Stella' – bears not only fruits but also enchanting spring blossom.

FIGS

Plant two year old fan-trained trees. Follow the training method used for peach fans.

ESTABLISHED FIGS   In spring remove all frost damaged, crowded or crossing stems. In summer pinch back young shoots to five leaves and remove surplus shoots.

RASPBERRIES

AUTUMN-FRUITING TYPES
Prune all fruited canes to
ground level in late winter
and tie in new canes as
they develop.

SUMMER-FRUITING TYPES
After planting prune each
cane to about 30cm/12in
above ground level.
Remove the old stumps
when new canes appear.
Prune established
summer-fruiting
raspberries after cropping
in autumn (shown left).
Prune all fruited canes to
ground level. Tie in strong
new canes as they develop,
spacing them 10cm/4in
apart. Thin out weak
growth. In late winter cut
back the dead cane tips to
just above the top wire.

GOOSEBERRIES

After planting shorten all branch leaders by half. Remove any suckers at ground level.
ESTABLISHED BUSHES   In summer shorten all side-shoots to five leaves (shown right). In winter shorten all side shoots to two buds and shorten all leaders by half.

REDCURRANTS AND WHITECURRANTS

After planting shorten all branch leaders by half. Prune to an outward facing bud. Remove dead, weak and crossing stems. Also cut out suckers and any shoots that develop on the leg.
ESTABLISHED BUSHES   In summer shorten sideshoots to five leaves (shown right) but do not shorten leaders. In winter cut back side-shoots to two buds and shorten leaders by half. Remove any dead, diseased or damaged stems. Old unproductive branches may be cut back to vigorous new growth.

BLACKCURRANTS

Immediately after planting, hard prune all shoots back to just above ground level, encouraging strong new shoots to develop.
Prune established bushes after leaf fall in autumn (before and after shown left). Remove up to a third of old fruited stems at ground level. Cut out weak shoots and damaged or badly placed branches.

BLACKBERRIES AND HYBRID BERRIES

After planting cut all stems down to about 25cm/10in above ground level. Tie in new shoots as they develop.
ESTABLISHED PLANTS Immediately after fruiting prune all fruited canes to ground level. Train and tie in the new canes onto training wires.
ALTERNATE BAY TRAINING Train last season's fruiting canes to one side of the plant and the new season's canes on the other side.
FAN TRAINING   Train fruiting canes to alternate sides and tie in the new season's canes in the centre gap.

BLUEBERRIES

In late winter prune two or three of the older unproductive branches to ground level or vigorous new growth. Remove dead, diseased or damaged stems.

4. HEDGES

These are the living walls of a garden. They divide and shape it, obscure and reveal it.

SHAPING HEDGES

HEDGES SERVE A RANGE OF USEFUL FUNCTIONS in the garden. They provide shelter from strong winds, screen less attractive views, ensure privacy, or they can be used to divide the garden into rooms. Hedges can also become attractive features in their own right.

When choosing hedging plants the climate, soil conditions and rates of growth should be considered. Fast growers, such as Leyland cypress will need cutting several times each summer. Slow-growing plants, such as yew, will need only one cut a year. Select formal hedging plants which have a dense habit of gowth and are tolerant of regular clipping. Informal hedging plants should maintain their shape with minimal pruning.

WHEN TO CUT HEDGES

Most hedges can be cut safely between late spring and late summer. Avoid cutting hedges later than this period since newly cut shoots can be damaged by frost, leading to die-back. For specific plants see individual entries for the ideal pruning or clipping times.

Hedges can be embellished with a range of decorative shapes. Hedge tops may be surmounted by topiary or battlements, the ends shaped into pillars or domes. Windows, arches or portholes cut into hedges would allow glimpses into other parts of the garden.

SHAPING HEDGES

Hedges should be shaped with gently sloping sides so that the top is narrower than the base. This will prevent lower branches being self-shaded and gradually dying back to produce a leafless base. The result will be a stronger well furnished hedge. Rounded or chamfered tops will help to prevent snow settling.

GOOD HEDGE SHAPES prevent self-shading and shed snow easily.

POOR HEDGE SHAPES – self-shading results in bare bases. Liable to snow damage.

CUTTING HEDGES

Once the hedge shape has been established, hedges need regular clipping to maintain their shape. Clip hedges with shears or an electric trimmer. These should be used with blades parallel to the hedge, not pointing into it.

Well defined hedges may be clipped straight by eye; otherwise a guiding line should be used.

Stretch a line between two posts at the correct height and level, then cut the hedge along this line. Clear all clippings from the hedge and then clip the sides and end.

Large leaved shrubs such as laurel should be pruned with secateurs because leaves sliced by shears turn brown and look unsightly.

RENOVATING HEDGES

A number of hedging plants, such as box (*Buxus*), hornbeam (*Carpinus*) and yew (*Taxus baccata*), can be renovated if they have become overgrown or neglected. Evergreen shrubs should be renovated in spring and deciduous types in winter, but coniferous hedges (other than yew) will not tolerate severe pruning.

In the first year prune only the top and one side of the hedge. Cut all branches back to the main stem or stems and prune the top back to the desired height. The following year cut back all branches on the other side.

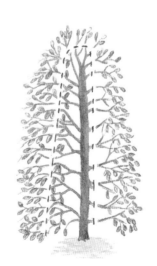

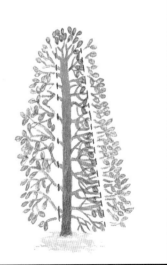

FORMAL HEDGES

FORMAL HEDGES have a strong architectural shape which defines the structure of a garden. They provide an ideal backcloth for garden ornaments or flowering plants. Formal hedges must be clipped regularly to maintain a close-textured surface.

A large box hedge acts as a wall beside a staircase in a large public garden. This has been clipped regularly to form a close texture and give the impression of solidity.

◆ *The dome emphasizes the architectural qualities of formal hedges of this kind.*

The buttresses on this yew hedge provide sunny enclosures for both the seat and the beds of day lilies.

A yew hedge has been turned into a grand entrance arch in this cottage garden, which also boasts spectacular topiary.

Hedge as topiary. This hedge of *Lonicera nitida* has been trimmed into a dragon.

FORMATIVE PRUNING

Initial pruning of formal hedges encourages bushy growth resulting in a dense, well furnished hedge.
1. After planting cut back all stems by about a third.
2. In the second winter cut back all stems by a third.
3. In the third summer begin clipping the sides to the desired shape. Clip the top lightly until the required height is reached.

CUTTING ESTABLISHED HEDGES

In subsequent years clip regularly to maintain the shape. See individual entries for the ideal clipping times of specific plants.

A retreat made in box. Formal hedges can be used in many imaginative ways to create features in even small gardens.

◆ *Box takes a long time to grow this high and dense, but its slowness means that it does not quickly become unmanageable.*

FORMAL DECIDUOUS HEDGES

Hornbeam (*Carpinus betulus*) Clip to maintain shape in late summer. Overgrown hedges may be rejuvenated by cutting back hard if necessary.

Beech (*Fagus sylvatica*) Clip to shape in late summer. Neglected or overgrown hedges may be rejuvenated by hard pruning in winter.

Hawthorn (*Crataegus monogyna*) Clip to shape in summer. Hawthorns respond to hard pruning. Cut back hedges in winter if necessary.

◆ *You feel beckoned to enter this garden by the glimpse through the arch.*

Box (*Buxus sempervirens*)
Box responds to regular clipping from late spring to late summer. Hard prune overgrown hedges in spring.

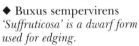

◆ Buxus sempervirens *'Suffruticosa' is a dwarf form used for edging.*

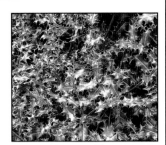

Holly (*Ilex aquifolium*)
Hedges should be pruned to shape in late summer. Overgrown hedges respond to hard pruning in spring.

Privet (*Ligustrum ovalifolium*) Clip regularly from spring to autumn. Overgrown hedges can be cut back hard in spring.

Lonicera nitida Clip regularly from spring to autumn to maintain shape. Overgrown hedges may be cut back hard if necessary.

Laurel (*Prunus laurocerasus*) Prune to shape with secateurs in spring or summer. Overgrown hedges respond to hard cutting back in spring.

◆ *These delicate candles of flowers appear in spring if you do not trim off the buds.*

CONIFERS AS HEDGES

CONIFERS MAKE EXCELLENT DENSE EVERGREEN HEDGES. They include the fast growing Leyland cypress (x *Cupressocyparis leylandii*), the slower growing yew (*Taxus baccata*) and many attractive cultivars of Lawson's cypress (*Chamaecyparis lawsoniana*) and Western red cedar (*Thuja plicata*). Coniferous hedges need regular clipping to maintain a well defined shape and prevent them outgrowing their situation.

1.

2.

FORMATIVE PRUNING

1. After planting shorten any long or straggly shoots, but leave the leader unpruned.

2. In the second summer clip side growth to the desired shape. Allow the leader to grow 30cm/12in above the required height, then prune 15cm/6in below it to promote side growth and the formation of a solid top.

Lawson's cypress
(*Chamaecyparis lawsoniana*)
When the desired height is
reached cut back the
leading shoot. Clip to
maintain shape in summer.

Yew (*Taxus baccata*) Clip to
maintain shape in summer.
Overgrown hedges may be
rejuvenated by hard cutting
back in spring.

Western red cedar (*Thuja
plicata*) Clip to shape in
summer. It will not tolerate
severe pruning.

Leyland cypress (x *Cupressocyparis
leylandii*) Clip to shape in late
spring and late summer. Avoid
cutting back into old wood.

CONIFERS
AS HEDGES

Western hemlock (*Tsuga
heterophylla*) Clip to
maintain shape in summer.
Avoid cutting back into old
wood.

CUTTING
ESTABLISHED HEDGES

Slower growing conifers
need only one cut in
summer. Faster growing
plants such as Leyland
cypress need two cuts a
year, in late spring and late
summer. Avoid cutting
coniferous hedges between
late autumn and early
spring.

INFORMAL DECIDUOUS HEDGES

A NUMBER OF SHRUBS make attractive and useful informal hedges. Such hedges provide effective barriers and there is the bonus of attractive flowers or fruit. Flowering and fruiting shrubs should be pruned to shape with secateurs immediately after flowering or fruiting. Remove any old wood or untidy growth.

Fuchsia Prune all stems to ground level in spring.

◆ *In mild districts prune to shape and remove frost damage.*

Berberis thunbergii Prune to maintain shape in late summer.

Forsythia Prune after flowering. Remove old and dead branches at ground level.

Potentilla In spring remove old and weak stems and shorten back strong new growth.

Prunus cerasifera After flowering remove old flowering stems and shorten back vigorous growth.

Rosa rugosa In spring remove old stems at ground level and shorten back vigorous shoots to maintain shape.

Spiraea × vanhouttei, and *S. thunbergii* Clip to maintain shape after flowering in early summer.

Symphoricarpus Thin out old and weak stems in early spring. Clip to maintain shape in summer.

Syringa (Lilac) No regular pruning. Overgrown hedges may be hard pruned after flowering.

Rosmarinus (Rosemary) Prune lightly to shape after flowering.

Santolina (Cotton lavender) (*right*) In spring cut off old flower stems and 2.5–5cm/1–2in of the previous year's growth. Overgrown bushes may be hard pruned.

Berberis darwinii Prune immediately after flowering. Cut back untidy or flowered stems using secateurs.

Cotoneaster lacteus Prune lightly to shape after fruiting in early winter. Overgrown hedges may be hard pruned in spring.

Escallonia rubra var. *macrantha* Prune to shape after flowering in midsummer. Shorten back frost damaged stems in spring.

Euonymus japonicus Prune lightly to maintain shape in spring. Cut out reverted shoots in variegated forms.

Griselinia littoralis Cut back frost damaged shoots in spring. Prune lightly to shape in summer.

Lavender In spring cut off dead flower stems and 2.5–5cm/1–2in of last year's growth. Avoid cutting into old wood.

Pyracantha (Firethorn) Prune lightly to maintain shape in summer.

Rhododendron No regular pruning. Prune lightly to maintain shape in summer. Overgrown hedges may be hard pruned after flowering.

◆ *This is* Rhododendron ponticum, *an invasive shrub which needs control.*

5. ROSES, WALL SHRUBS, CLIMBERS, SUB-SHRUBS

As well as roses there are important subjects for pruning in this chapter.

ROSES

THE PURPOSE OF PRUNING ROSES is to remove damaged, dead and unproductive stems to encourage the development of vigorous new shoots.

WHEN TO PRUNE

Most roses should be pruned in early spring before they start to grow. Pruning any earlier may result in die-back due to frost damage.

In the autumn shorten long shoots to prevent the plants suffering from wind-rock during winter and complete the pruning process in spring.

Dead-head roses regularly in summer.

DEAD-HEADING

Cutting off the dead flowers (dead-heading) regularly throughout the summer will prolong the flowering period. Cut back to the first strong bud or shoot.

PRUNING BASICS

1. Prune dead, diseased and weak, spindly growth back to a healthy bud or stem or to ground level.

2. Aim to produce an open-centred bush. Remove any crossing or inward-growing stems. Prune back to outward-facing buds.

3. Make clean, sloping cuts slightly above outward-facing buds.

4. Remove suckering shoots when they appear. Trace the sucker back to the root and pull it off. Don't cut it off at ground level as this will only encourage more suckers.

Prune the remaining stems according to the rose type.

HYBRID TEA ROSES
(Large-flowered Bush Roses)

In early spring, completely remove dead, diseased or damaged stems. Cut out crossing and overcrowded stems and prune all those that remain to about 30cm/1ft above ground level. Dead-head regularly throughout the summer. In late autumn shorten long shoots.

FLORIBUNDA
(Cluster-flowered Bush Roses)

Floribunda roses are pruned like Hybrid Teas, but since they are more vigorous and free-flowering, their pruning does not need to be so severe.

In early spring, cut out completely all dead, diseased or damaged stems. Prune each of the main stems to about 30cm/1ft above the ground. Shorten the side shoots to about 15cm/6in.

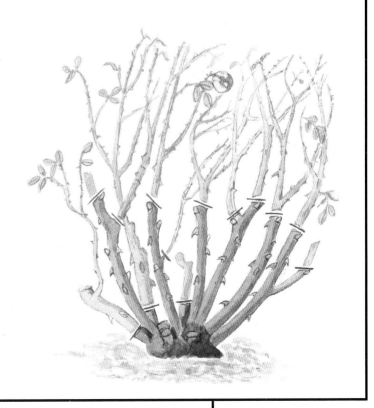

STANDARD ROSES

(Hybrid Tea and Floribunda)

Remove dead, twiggy and overcrowded stems from the centre. Shorten stems by about one third so that the main branches are of equal length, forming a balanced head.

WEEPING STANDARDS

After blooming, remove all the stems that have flowered.

MINIATURE AND PATIO ROSES

Remove dead, diseased and twiggy growth. Shorten vigorous shoots to half their length.

SHRUB ROSES

In early spring, remove weak and badly positioned branches. Every year cut out two or three of the oldest branches from the base. Shorten vigorous shoots by about one third of their length.

RAMBLER ROSES

After blooming, prune all stems that have flowered to ground level. Train and tie in new shoots as they develop.

CLIMBING ROSES

In early spring, remove dead, diseased or weak growth. Cut back sideshoots that have flowered to about 7.5cm/3in long. Tie in strong new shoots as they develop in summer. A little later in the spring, train and tie these into their permanent positions.

SPECIES ROSES

These don't need to be pruned regularly. When necessary, remove dead or diseased stems. Cut out old and weak branches on mature specimens to encourage vigorous new growth.

Abutilon Remove frosted or dead growth in spring. Cut off old flower heads.

◆ *Shown here is* Abutilon × suntense.

Azara Requires little pruning. Unwanted shoots should be cut back to the framework in spring. E

Callistemon (Bottlebrush) No regular pruning. Remove old branches back to ground level in spring. E

Cytisus battandieri No regular pruning. Remove dead and damaged growth in spring. Semi-E

◆ *This is known as the pineapple broom because of its scent.*

Carpenteria No regular pruning. Shorten straggly branches after flowering. Older branches may be removed occasionally to stimulate new growth. E

Drimys No regular pruning. Prune damaged stems back to new growth in spring. E

× **Fatshedera** No regular pruning. Remove damaged stems in spring. E

A NUMBER OF SHRUBS can be trained against walls. Not only can they be shown to their best advantage, but walls provide shelter and warmth for tender shrubs.

Fremontodendron No regular pruning. Remove dead and damaged shoots in spring. Semi-E

◆ *A vigorous bush with showy flowers from late spring into autumn.*

Itea No regular pruning. Remove old or dead wood in spring. E

◆ *The tassels of small flowers appear in late summer.*

Myrtus (Myrtle) No regular pruning. Remove straggly growth and frost damage in spring. E

WALL SHRUBS

FORMING THE FRAMEWORK

In spring tie in the leader vertically. Spread out and tie in side growths. Remove badly placed shoots and cut breastwood (outward-growing stems) back to 5–7.5cm/2–3in.
In summer continue training and tying-in growth until all space is filled. Remove badly placed or crossing shoots. Prune breastwood back to 7.5–10cm/3–4in.

PRUNING ESTABLISHED PLANTS

After flowering cut back all breastwood to within 10cm/4in of the framework. Continue tying in shoots as they develop.
Avoid cutting back wall shrubs after midsummer since soft growth may develop, which is liable to frost damage.

Garrya (Tassel bush) and *Pyracantha* (Firethorn) are also grown as wall shrubs.

CLIMBERS

ONCE ESTABLISHED, many climbers need little pruning except for the removal of dead and diseased wood. However, climbers trained over pergolas, arches and restricted areas need regular pruning to restrict growth and encourage the development of flowers.

INITIAL PRUNING

Train the strongest stems to the support in a fan formation, leaving space between each stem. Remove weak and unwanted stems completely. The following spring cut back sideshoots to six buds and shorten back excessively vigorous leaders.

PRUNING ESTABLISHED CLIMBERS

Climbers which flower on the current season's wood are pruned in spring. Remove dead and damaged stems. Thin out crowded stems and shorten back sideshoots.
Climbers which flower on the previous year's wood should be pruned after flowering. Prune flowered shoots back to new growth. Remove dead, damaged and twiggy growth. Self-clinging climbers, such as ivy (*Hedera*) need little attention except to restrain growth.

Actinidia When the allotted space is covered, shorten growth back to 15–23cm/6–9in in early winter.

Akebia No regular pruning. Remove dead and weak growth in spring.

Ampelopsis Once a framework of main stems has been established, prune annual growth back to two buds after leaf fall.

Aristolochia (Dutchman's pipe) No regular pruning. Remove any dead or unwanted growth in spring.

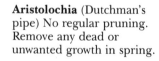

Campsis Prune last year's growth back to two or three buds in early spring.

CLEMATIS

SPRING-FLOWERING SPECIES AND CULTIVARS
(Clematis alpina, C. macropetala, C. montana, C. armandii and *C. cirrhosa)*
Prune these immediately after they have flowered. Cut back dead and damaged stems to a strong pair of buds. If the space where they grow is restricted, prune all the flowered stems to within 1 or 2 buds of the main framework.

EARLY LARGE-FLOWERED CULTIVARS
(For example, 'Nelly Moser', 'Vyvyan Pennell', 'The President', 'Niobe')
In early spring, remove dead and damaged stems. Cut back old and weak stems to a healthy pair of buds and tie in replacement stems.

LATE-FLOWERING SPECIES AND CULTIVARS
(C. florida, C × jackmanii, C. tangutica, C. texensis, C. viticella, 'Perle d'Azur', 'Hagley Hybrid')
In early spring, hard prune all the previous year's growth back to just above the base at strong leaf-axil buds.

CLIMBERS

Eccremocarpus (Glory vine) Prune damaged stems back to new growth in spring.

Hedera (Ivy) No routine pruning. Cut back excessive growth in early summer.

Jasminum (Jasmine) No regular pruning. Cut out old stems after flowering. Tie in new shoots.

Hydrangea anomala ssp. *petiolaris*
Shorten back unwanted growth in summer.

◆ *This climber makes a slow start but grows rapidly once established.*

Lonicera (Honeysuckle) After flowering, shorten flowered shoots back to new growth. Cut out some old stems.

Parthenocissus Cut back growth in autumn if it is necessary to restrict size.

Passiflora (Passion flower) In spring, remove dead stems at ground level. Thin out crowded stems and shorten side shoots back to 15cm/6in.

Schizophragma No regular pruning. Prune back dead or unwanted growth and remove old flower heads in the autumn.

Solanum In spring, shorten weak growth and cut back last year's shoots to 15cm/6in. Tie in new growth throughout the summer.

Trachelospermum No regular pruning. Thin out unwanted growth in spring. Shorten back vigorous shoots.

Vitis (Grapevine) No regular pruning. In restricted spaces, prune back to two buds from the framework after leaf fall.

Wisteria In summer, prune long growth back to four or five leaves. In winter, shorten back to two buds.

SUB-SHRUBS

Tender sub-shrubs such as cistus can be severely damaged in hard winters. Leave the damaged growth intact until the spring and prune back to new growth.

Some sub-shrubs such as helianthemum, thyme and erica should be pruned after flowering. Cut back just below the faded flower spikes.

IF LEFT UNATTENDED sub-shrubs become leggy and produce fewer flowers. Regular pruning promotes strong bushy growth. Sub-shrubs are liable to frost damage, so pruning should be delayed until late spring when the danger of severe frost has passed.

Artemisia Hard prune *A. abrotanum* and *A. absinthium* in spring. Other species, remove frost damage and straggly growth.

Ballota Cut back all growth by half in spring to maintain a compact shape.

Caryopteris Hard prune back to new growth in spring.

Cistus Shorten straggly growths, remove dead and frost damaged branches in spring. Avoid cutting into old wood.

Dorycnium Prune dead stems back to new growth in spring.

Erica (Heath) Clip over with shears after flowering to remove faded flowers and promote compact growth.

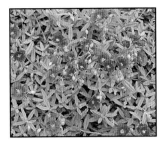

Helianthemum (Rock rose) Cut back with shears after flowering to encourage compact growth.

Lavender Clip over bushes in spring. Shorten by 2.5cm/1in to stimulate new growth. Avoid pruning into old wood.

Rosemary Prune back winter damage to new growth in late spring. Also shorten long straggly growths.

Rue Hard prune back to new growth near the base in spring. Remove weak growth.

Thyme Shorten growth by half after flowering to maintain a compact shape.

Sage Remove old and damaged stems in spring. Leggy plants may be hard pruned back to new growth.

Santolina (Cotton lavender) Trim after flowering to remove old flower stems or, for foliage effect, prune to new growth in spring.

Vinca (Periwinkle) No regular pruning. Vincas may occasionally be hard pruned to ground level in early spring.

GLOSSARY

Breastwood Shoots on a wall-trained shrub which grow away from the wall.

Cordon A plant, normally a fruiting shrub or tree, which is trained to a single upright or slanting stem against a support. However, double and triple-stemmed cordons are also grown.

Current growth Growth that is made during the current year.

Dead-head Removal of the dead flowers from a plant.

Die-back The tip of the shoot starts to blacken and die, the disease spreading back along the stem to the base.

Epicormic shoots These shoots (water shoots) arise from latent or adventitious buds which form just under the bark of woody plants. If the trunk or main stem is damaged, they break out of the bark and grow.

Espalier A shrub or tree (usually fruiting), the side-stems of which have been trained to grow horizontally in tiers along supports.

Fan-trained A shrub or tree (usually fruiting) which has been trained into the shape of a radiating fan.

Fastigiate A plant of erect, very narrow habit.

Feathered A young tree with shoots growing off the side of its main stem.

Lateral A side growth (or side shoot) on a shrub or tree.

Leader The stem or leading shoot that is dominant on a shrub or tree. It is usually the central top one and, if undamaged, extends the plant vertically.

Leg The part of the main stem of a tree or shrub from the ground to the lowest branch.

Maiden A tree which is in its first year after being budded or grafted.

Pollard The cutting back at intervals of branches to a stem or framework.

Reversion Returning to the original form, as when variegated leaves revert to green.

Spur A short stem with clusters of flower or fruit buds.

Spur-bearing Varieties of trees or bushes which bear fruit on spurs are called spur-bearing.

Standard A standard shrub is one whose stem has been stripped of side growths so that shoots appear at the top of a clear stem.

Sub-lateral A sideshoot from a lateral shoot or branch.

Sub-shrub This refers to either a plant with a woody base and soft herbaceous growth above, or a low-growing plant that is fully woody.

Sucker A shoot coming from below the ground originating on the plant's roots or underground stem. It is also used to refer to a shoot originating from beneath the graft union on a grafted plant.

Tip-bearing Varieties of trees or bushes which bear fruit on the tips of their shoots are called tip-bearing.

Water shoots See Epicormic shoots.

INDEX OF PLANTS

Brachyglottis See
  Senecio
Bramble 18 and see Rubus
Broom See Cytisus and
  Genista
Buddleja alternifolia 12, 16,
  23
  B. davidii 12, 18, 23
  B. globosa 23
Butterfly bush See *Buddleja
  davidii*
Buxus 16, 23, 55, 59
  B. sempervirens
    'Suffruticosa' 59

Californian lilac See
  Ceanothus
Calico bush See Kalmia
Callistemon 70
Calluna 12
Camellia 23
Campsis 72
Carpenteria 70
Carpinus See Hornbeam
Caryopteris 12, 76
Castanea See Sweet chestnut
Catalpa See Indian bean
  tree
Ceanothus 12, 23
Ceratostigma 12, 23
Cercis See Judas tree
Chaenomeles 24
Chamaecyparis lawsoniana
  See Lawson's cypress
Cherry 12, 41, 49 and see
  Prunus
Chimonanthus 24
Choisya 24
Cinquefoil See Potentilla
Cistus 76
Clematis 12
  C. alpina 73
  C. armandii 73
  C. cirrhosa 73
  C. florida 73
  C. 'Hagley Hybrid' 73
  C. × jackmanii 73
  C. macropetala 73
  C. montana 73
  C. 'Nelly Moser' 73

C. 'Niobe' 73
C. 'Perle d'Azur' 73
C. tangutica 73
C. texensis 73
C. 'The President' 73
C. viticella 73
C. 'Vyvyan Pennell' 73
Clerodendrum 24
  C. bungei 24
  C. trichotomum 24
Cornus 12, 19, 24
  C. alba 10, 18, 24
Corylus See Hazel
  C. avellana 38
  C. colurna 38
  C. maxima 'Purpurea' 18
Cotinus 18, 25
Cotoneaster 25
  C. lacteus 63
Cotton lavender See
  Santolina
Crab apple 39
Crataegus See Hawthorn
× *Cupressocyparis leylandii*
  See Leyland cypress
Cytisus 17, 25
  C. battandieri 70

Daboecia 12
Daisy bush See Olearia
Daphne 25
Day lily 57
Deutzia 12, 16, 25
Dogwood 10, 18 and see
  Cornus
Dorycnium 76
Drimys 71
Dutchman's pipe See
  Aristolochia

Eccremocarpus 74
Elaeagnus 12, 25
Elder 18 and see Sambucus
Elm 41
Erica 12, 76
Escallonia 26
  E. rubra var. *macrantha* 63
Eucalyptus 12, 18, 19, 38
Euonymus 26
  E. japonicus 63

Exochorda 26

Fagus See Beech
False acacia 41 and see
  Robinia
False castor oil plant See
  Fatsia
× Fatshedera 71
Fatsia 26
Fig 49
Firethorn See Pyracantha
Flowering currant See
  Ribes
Forsythia 12, 16, 17, 27, 62
Foxglove tree 39 and see
  Paulownia
Fraxinus 38
Fremontodendron 71
Fuchsia 12, 18, 27, 62

Gage 12, 48, 49
Garrya 27, 71
Gaultheria See Pernettya
Genista 17, 27
Gleditsia See Honey locust
Glory vine See
  Eccremocarpus
Golden rain 39 and see
  Laburnum
Gooseberry 12, 51
Grapevine See Vitis
Griselinia littoralis 63

Hamamelis 27
Hardy plumbago See
  Ceratostigma
Hawthorn 38
Hazel 38
Heath See Erica
Heather 13, 17
Hebe 12, 27
Hedera 72, 74
Helianthemum 13, 76, 77
Hibiscus 27
Hippophaë 28
Holly 39, 59
Honey locust 39
Honeysuckle See
  Lonicera
Hornbeam 38, 55

Horse chestnut 12, 38
Hydrangea 12, 28
  H. anomala ssp. *petiolaris* 74
  H. macrophylla 28
  H. paniculata 18, 19, 28
Hypericum 12, 18, 28
  H. calycinum 28
  H. × inodorum 28

Ilex See Holly
Indian bean tree 38
Indigo bush See Indigofera
Indigofera 28
Itea 71
Ivy 11 and see *Hedera*

Japanese quince See
  Chaenomeles
Jasmine See Jasminum
Jasminum 74
  J. nudiflorum 12, 16
Jerusalem sage See
  Phlomis
Judas tree 38
Juglans See Walnut

Kalmia 28
Kerria 16, 29
Koelreuteria See Pride of
  India
Kolkwitzia 12, 16, 29

Laburnum 12
Laurel 16, 22, 55 and see
  Prunus
Lavatera 12, 29
Lavender 63, 77
Lawson's cypress 60, 61
Leptospermum 29
Leucothoë 29
Leycesteria 12, 18, 30
Leyland cypress 54, 60, 61
Ligustrum ovalifolium See
  Privet
Lilac See Syringa
Lime 19, 41
Liquidambar See Sweet gum
Liriodendron See Tulip tree
Lonicera 30, 57, 74
  L. nitida 16, 22, 57, 59